my child is

____

born on

____

when?
age?
where?
what you said?

when? ___

age? ___

where? ___

what you said?

when? ____________________

age? ____________________

where? ____________________

what you said?

when? ______________________

age? ______________________

where? ______________________

what you said?

when?
age?
where?
what you said?

when?
age?
where?
what you said?

when? ______________________________

age? ______________________________

where? ______________________________

what you said?

when?
age?
where?
what you said?

when?
age?
where?
what you said?

when? ______________________

age? ______________________

where? ______________________

what you said?

when? ______________________

age? ______________________

where? ______________________

what you said?

when?
age?
where?
what you said?

when?
age?
where?
what you said?

when? ____________________

age? ____________________

where? ____________________

what you said?

when? ______________________

age? ______________________

where? ______________________

what you said?

when?
age?
where?
what you said?

when?
age?
where?
what you said?

when? ______________________

age? ______________________

where? ______________________

what you said?

when? ______________________

age? ______________________

where? ______________________

what you said?

when? ______________________

age? ______________________

where? ______________________

what you said?

when?
age?
where?
what you said?

when? ______________________

age? ______________________

where? ______________________

what you said?

when?

age?

where?

what you said?

when?
age?
where?
what you said?

when?
age?
where?
what you said?

when? ______

age? ______

where? ______

what you said?

when? ______________________

age? ______________________

where? ______________________

what you said?

when? ___________

age? ___________

where? ___________

what you said?

when?
age?
where?
what you said?

when?
age?
where?
what you said?

when? ______________________

age? ______________________

where? ______________________

what you said?

when?
age?
where?
what you said?

when?
age?
where?
what you said?

when?
age?
where?
what you said?

when?
age?
where?
what you said?

when?
age?
where?
what you said?

when?
age?
where?
what you said?

when? ____________________

age? ____________________

where? ____________________

what you said?

when? ______________________

age? ______________________

where? ______________________

what you said?

when?
age?
where?
what you said?

when?

age?

where?

what you said?

when? ______________________

age? ______________________

where? ______________________

what you said?

when? ______________________

age? ______________________

where? ______________________

what you said?

when?
age?
where?
what you said?

when?
age?
where?
what you said?

when?
age?
where?
what you said?

when? ______________________

age? ______________________

where? ______________________

what you said?

when?
age?
where?
what you said?

when?
age?
where?
what you said?

when?
age?
where?
what you said?

when? ______________________

age? ______________________

where? ______________________

what you said?

when? ____________________

age? ____________________

where? ____________________

what you said?

when?
age?
where?
what you said?

when?
age?
where?
what you said?

when? ___________________

age? ___________________

where? ___________________

what you said?

when?
age?
where?
what you said?

when?
age?
where?
what you said?

when? ______________________

age? ______________________

where? ______________________

what you said?

when? ____________________

age? ____________________

where? ____________________

what you said?

when?
age?
where?
what you said?

when?
age?
where?
what you said?

when?
age?
where?
what you said?

when? ____________________

age? ____________________

where? ____________________

what you said?

when?
age?
where?
what you said?

when?
age?
where?
what you said?

when?
age?
where?
what you said?

when? ___

age? ___

where? ___

what you said?

when?
age?
where?
what you said?

when?
age?
where?
what you said?

when?
age?
where?
what you said?

when? ____________________

age? ____________________

where? ____________________

what you said?

when?
age?
where?
what you said?

when?
age?
where?
what you said?

when?
age?
where?
what you said?

when? ______________________

age? ______________________

where? ______________________

what you said?

when?
age?
where?
what you said?

when?
age?
where?
what you said?

when?
age?
where?
what you said?

when? ______________________

age? ______________________

where? ______________________

what you said?

when?
age?
where?
what you said?

when?
age?
where?
what you said?

when?
age?
where?
what you said?

when? ______________________

age? ______________________

where? ______________________

what you said?

when?
age?
where?
what you said?

when?
age?
where?
what you said?

when?
age?
where?
what you said?

when? ______________________

age? ______________________

where? ______________________

what you said?

when?
age?
where?
what you said?

when?
age?
where?
what you said?

when?
age?
where?
what you said?

when?

age?

where?

what you said?

when?
age?
where?
what you said?

when?
age?
where?
what you said?

when?
age?
where?
what you said?

when? ______________________

age? ______________________

where? ______________________

what you said?

when? ______________________

age? ______________________

where? ______________________

what you said?

24046833R00058

Made in the USA
San Bernardino, CA
02 February 2019